# SCHOOL TIMES

## TIMES

### A SPOT-IT CHALLENGE

by Jennifer L. Marks

Capstone press®

Mankato, Minnesota

A+ books

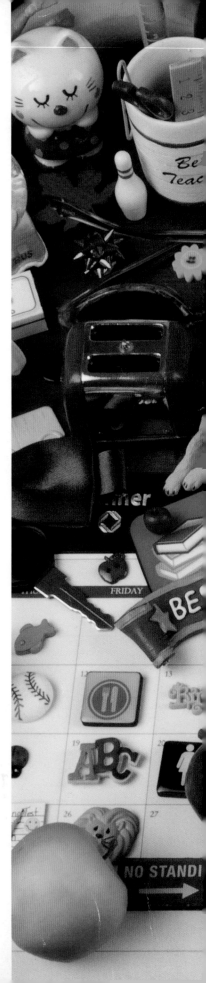

A+ Books are published by Capstone Press,
151 Good Counsel Drive, P.O. Box 669, Mankato, Minnesota 56002.
www.capstonepress.com

1  2  3  4  5  6   14  13  12  11  10  09

*Library of Congress Cataloging-in-Publication Data*
Marks, Jennifer, 1979–
    School times : a spot-it challenge / by Jennifer L. Marks.
    p. cm. –  (A+ books. Spot it)
    Includes bibliographical references.
    Summary: "Simple text invites the reader to find items hidden in school-themed
photographs"–Provided by publisher.
    ISBN-13: 978-1-4296-2218-9 (hardcover)
    ISBN-10: 1-4296-2218-0 (hardcover)
    1. Picture puzzles — Juvenile literature. 2. Schools — Juvenile literature. I. Title. II. Series.
GV1507.P47M275 2009
793.73–dc22                                          2008046827

Credits
Juliette Peters, set designer
Len Epstein, illustrator
All photos by Capstone Press Photo Studio.

Note to Parents, Teachers, and Librarians
Spot It is an interactive series that supports literacy development and reading enjoyment. Readers
utilize visual discrimination skills to find objects among fun-to-peruse photographs with busy
backgrounds. Readers also build vocabulary through thematic groupings, develop visual memory
ability through repeated readings, and improve strategic and associative thinking skills by
experimenting with different visual search methods.

The author dedicates this book to two of her high school teachers, Mr. Bryon Ubl and Mr. Larry Tise.

092009
005605R

# Table of Contents

First Stop: My Locker .....................4

Assignments Due on My Desk .........6

"P" Is for Pickle..............................8

Weird Science ...............................10

Good Sports ..................................12

You Gonna Eat That?.....................14

Recess, at Last!.............................16

A Whiteboard Class-tastrophy ....18

We Heart Art .................................20

And the Band Marches On ...........22

Totally Busted!..............................24

The Dog Ate My Homework...........26


Spot Even More!...........................28

Extreme Spot-It Challenge ............31

Read More .....................................32

Internet Sites................................32

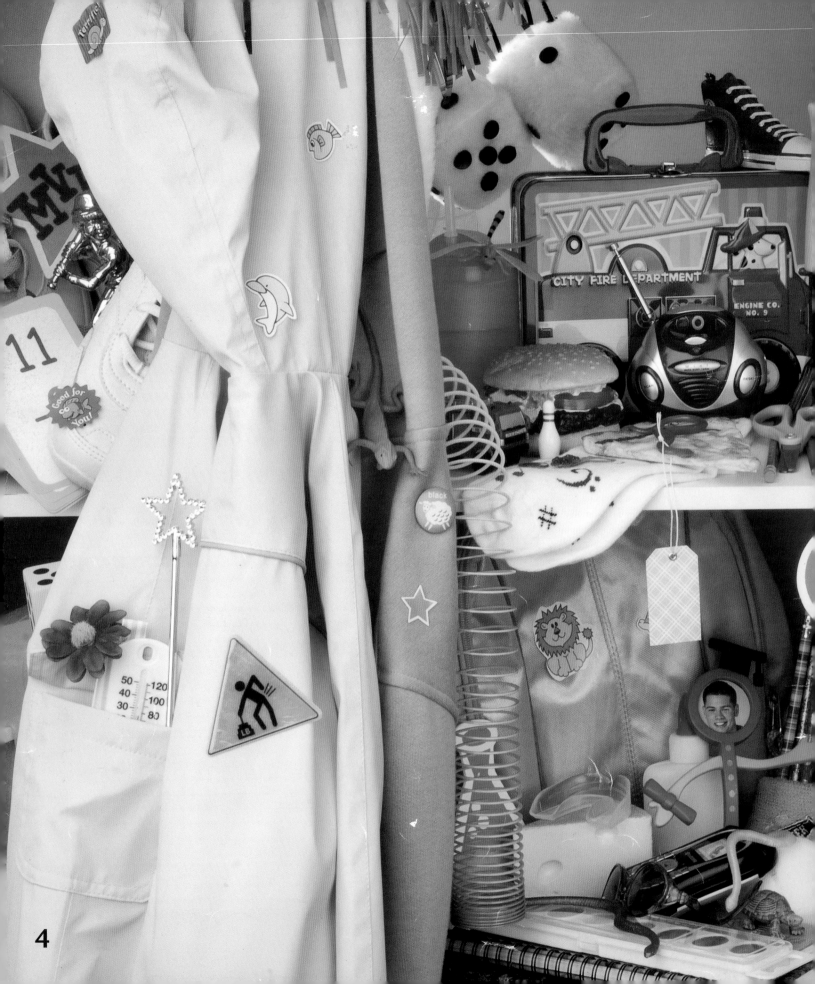

# First Stop: My Locker

Can you spot . . .

- a tortoise?
- a lizard?
- a trophy?
- a comb?
- a bowling pin?
- a green car?

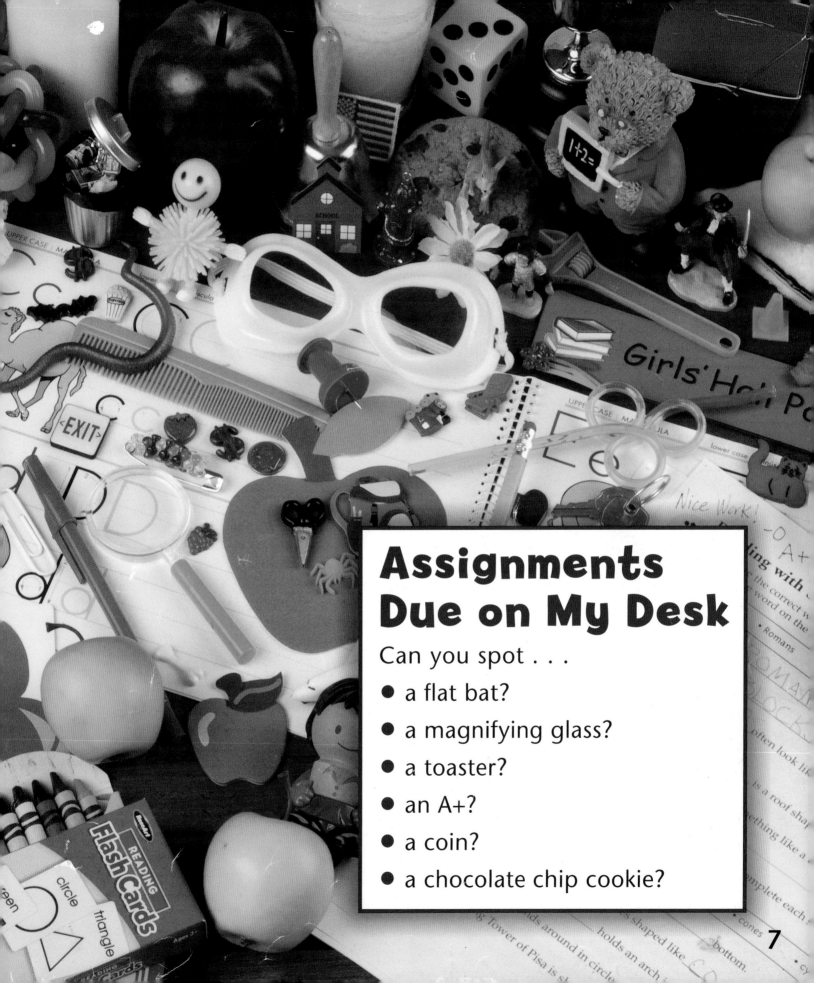

# Assignments Due on My Desk

Can you spot . . .

- a flat bat?
- a magnifying glass?
- a toaster?
- an A+?
- a coin?
- a chocolate chip cookie?

# "P" Is for Pickle

Can you spot . . .

- a tennis racquet?
- a giraffe?
- a trophy?
- a pickle?
- a slice of pizza?
- a rainbow?

# Weird Science

Can you spot . . .

- a rat?
- a mustache?
- five frogs?
- a windmill?
- a clover?
- a snake?

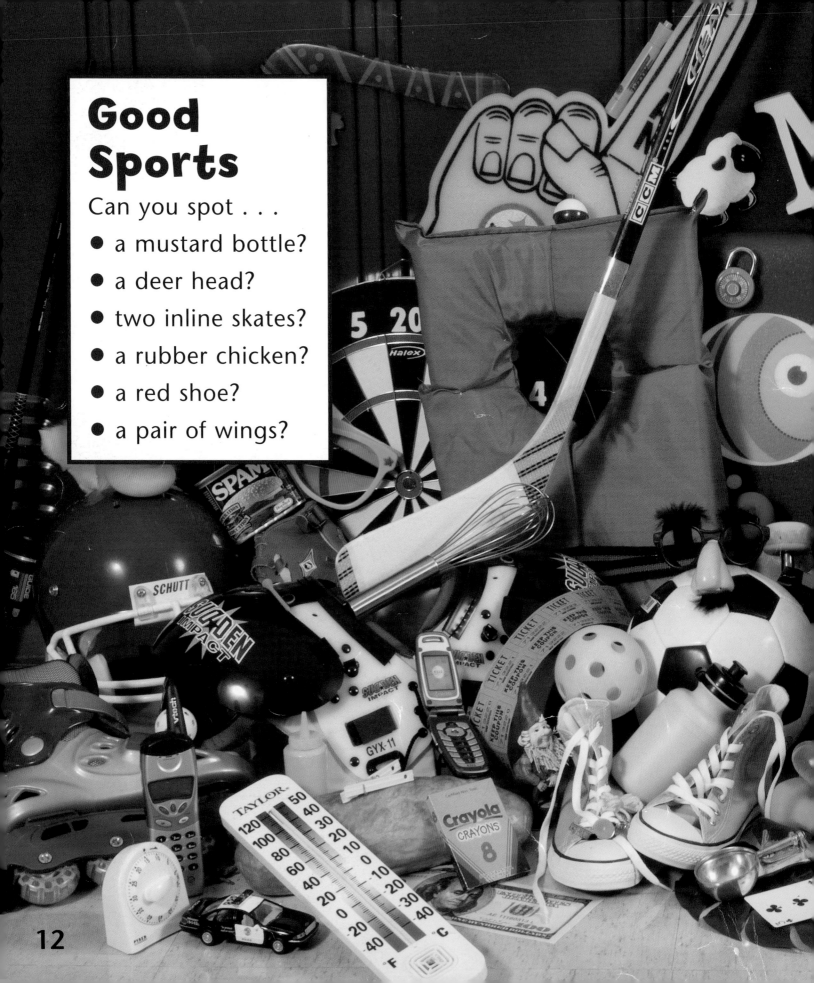

# Good Sports

Can you spot . . .

- a mustard bottle?
- a deer head?
- two inline skates?
- a rubber chicken?
- a red shoe?
- a pair of wings?

14

# You Gonna Eat That?

Can you spot . . .

- a tiny teddy bear?
- four croutons?
- a silver whistle?
- two ice cubes?
- a cowboy boot?
- a balloon?

# Recess, at Last!

Can you spot . . .

- a dragon?
- a hammer?
- an ear of corn?
- a football?
- a yellow button?
- a saddle?

16

# A Whiteboard Class-tastrophy

Can you spot . . .

- a jump rope?
- a big sneeze?
- eight sheep?
- two fish?
- a dribble of drool?
- a shepherd's cane?

# We Heart Art

Can you spot . . .

- a paper chain?
- a brown nest with eggs?
- a box of floss?
- a xylophone?
- a tiny panda?
- a unicorn?

# And the Band Marches On

Can you spot . . .

- chatty teeth?
- a triangle?
- a Slinky?
- a spotted flip-flop?
- a bunny?
- a sheriff's badge?

# Totally Busted!

Can you spot . . .

- an astronaut?
- two wads of gum?
- a cotton swab?
- barbecue sauce?
- a nail clipper?
- a little dog?

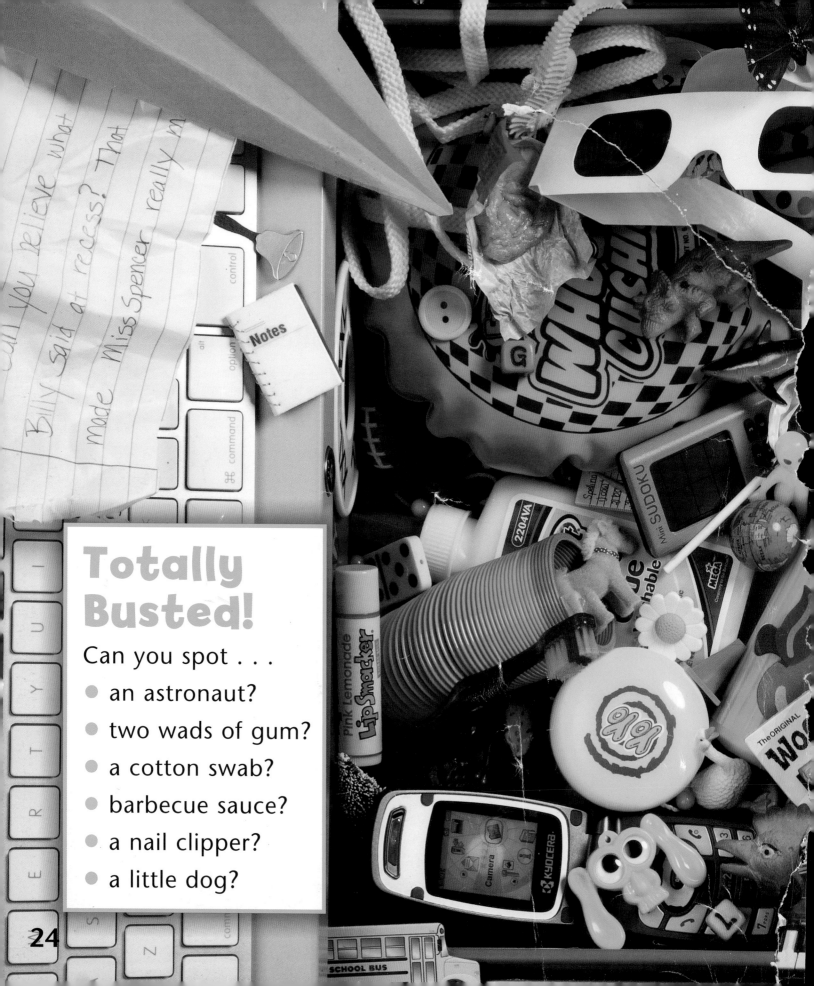

# The Dog Ate My Homework

Can you spot . . .

- a hot dog?
- a toothpick?
- a fuzzy duck?
- a sandwich?
- two combs?
- a bottle of glue?

# Spot Even More!

## First Stop: My Locker 4

See if you can spot a pink letter x, a blue snake, a carrot, a green lock, a paper crane, and a dragonfly.

## Assignments Due on My Desk 6

Try to find a ruler, a space shuttle, a cowbell, a mouse, and a banana.

## "P" Is for Pickle 8

Take another look and find a horseshoe, a blue eyeball, keys, a moose, a red shoe, and a blue house.

## Weird Science 10

Now find a box of popcorn, two white daisies, an ant, a pretzel, a tiny bone, and a gummy worm.

## Good Sports 12

Now spot a hundred dollar bill, two water bottles, three Wiffle balls, two goggles, a gnome, and a blue car.

## You Gonna Eat That? 14

Take another look and find a football helmet, a bunch of matches, a cockroach, and a construction cone.

### Recess, at Last! 16
See if you can find a golden crown, a scissors, a red sweatband, an alley cat, and purple sandals.

### A Whiteboard Class-tastrophy 18
Now spot a nose-picker, a bag of frogs, a mailbox, and a mouse hole.

### We Heart Art 20
Try to find a beehive, a blue ribbon, a blue button, a pumpkin, a pea pod, and a school bus.

### And the Band Marches On 22
Try to find a blue head, two pink shoes, a feather duster, and an army tank.

### Totally Busted! 24
Now look for a blue shark, a battleship, a deck of cards, a toothbrush, and a tiny yellow pencil.

### The Dog Ate My Homework 26
Try to spy a hiker, a spoon, a parrot, a bandage, a clothespin, and a snake.

29

# Extreme Spot-It Challenge

Just can't get enough Spot-It action? Try this extra credit challenge. See if you can spot:

- a bottle of glue
- a strand of pearls
- a three-leafed clover
- seven daisies
- five baseballs
- three zebras
- a yellow car
- a red pen
- two school buses
- a teddy bear
- two bunches of grapes
- two bunnies
- an orange fish
- a pinwheel
- three smiling skulls
- a bunch of carrots
- a spelling test

# Read More

**Kidslabel.** *School.* Spot 7. Seek & Find. San Francisco: Chronicle, 2006.

**Marks, Jennifer L.** *Mean Machines: A Spot-It Challenge.* Spot It. Mankato, Minn.: Capstone Publishers, 2009.

**Marzollo, Jean.** *I Spy a School Bus.* Scholastic Reader. New York: Scholastic, 2003.

# Internet Sites

FactHound offers a safe, fun way to find educator-approved Internet sites related to this book.

Here's what you do:

1. Visit *www.facthound.com*
2. Choose your grade level.
3. Begin your search.

This book's ID number is 9781429622189.

FactHound will fetch the best sites for you!